SPIRITUAL WARFARE
AND THE
BLENDED FAMILY

SPIRITUAL WARFARE AND THE BLENDED FAMILY

Dr. Jennie Morris, Th D

ISBN 979-8-218-65542-6

Printed in the United States of America

Publisher: Sophisticated Press
Publisher Consultant: Dr. Jennie Morris
Book Design: Sophisticated Press

*All scriptures are quoted from the King James Version Bible unless expressed otherwise.

SP
SOPHISTICATED
PRESS

ACKNOWLEDGMENTS

This book is dedicated to all families, particularly blended and extended families.

I want to dedicate this book to Mary Jean Eaglin and my stepdad, Willie Eaglin, who have passed away. They made the house a home.

To my two daughters, Yulonda Durst and Tiffany Perez, and three sons, Charles Williams Jr., David Morris (deceased), and Roderick Morris Sr., have shown me in so many ways that love will conquer no matter what the circumstances may be. You have taught me how to love my extended family through many years of living in a blended family. You showed me that it was more than words; it was from the heart. I will always be grateful for the lessons you taught me as you embraced your stepdad, Charles Morris Sr., and the children that came with him, Stephany, Charles Jr., and Derrick (deceased). I appreciate the ability that each one of you exhibited to make him and his children a part of our close-knit family. And because of that, I learned to feel what they felt and cared when they needed me to care. Thank you all for helping me overcome obstacles when I did not think I could.

To my sister, Delores Davis, whose blended family was so intertwined by the love you showed to all the children, treating each one as your biological child. I appreciate the example.

To my dear friend Diverna Abatte, you have been a foster parent as long as I've known you. It's a gift from God. You have shown so much love and compassion to the children in their time of heartache and pain after being separated from their parents. I watched you love those children and pray for them and their families. I saw the genuine love you gave them so they could heal and become whole while away from their parents. I watch as you protect each one from harmful words and rejections. And I also saw some of them come back to thank you when they grew up. Your love for the foster children was amazing. Thank you for expressing what unconditional love is.

And to all extended and blended families that have committed to make every effort to make the house a home for the family. I want to commend the blended families that have come together, even with the determination that the family will succeed. Also, it is essential to determine that the divorce statistics will not be a part of the number of the family. With the help of God, you know failure is not an option for your family; to those who have made up your mind through the power of the Holy Spirit, this family will succeed.

I pray that this book will help answer some of the questions and solve some of the problems you may encounter while building your blended and extended family, as you know it can be, with the help of God's Holy Spirit.

Sweet Memories

David DeVon Morris Sr.
November 21, 1979 - September 6, 2019

Derrick Dewayne Morris
May 8, 1977- September 2, 2000

Cherishing every sweet memory made with you.

Table of Contents

Introduction

I was in a blended family, so my heart is with the households that have come together to make a home. Not only was I raised in a blended family, but I was also raised in a family that had to blend. The trials and tribulations of uniting a family that had begun development in another relationship are a task. Indeed, we need the help of God through his Spirit to deal with the encounters and struggles that these new relationships bring.

In today's society, divorce is as common as eating. People come together in what is supposed to be holy matrimony. The idea is that they will live happily ever after with the person they are committing to. Sharing love and their life, they also choose to have a family. In this union, they are supposed to become one. But sometimes those plans fail. For various reasons, people change and no longer want to remain in a marriage or relationship. Some people choose not to deal with the struggles of marriage or a long-term relationship. Think that they are incompatible. Many times, people get married without a real commitment. Some may choose a lifestyle that brings other people into the marriage. These are known as swingers. Swingers are people who are married or in a long-term relationship and who like to have sex with other people's partners. But sometimes, one partner doesn't want that life any longer. It's either stay in it or divorce. You can also get a divorce because you want one. It is much easier now that a person can get a "no-fault" divorce. When we have that kind of non-committal marriage, you can expect marriages not to last. This is not God's intention for marriage. Children are born and even adopted and fostered in these marriages. God hates divorce.

God established marriage at the beginning of the creation. To accept, you must believe in God and his word. God established marriage in peace and harmony. There was no anger, arguments, or jealousy. God created Adam and Eve, and they realized they were one (Gen 2:23-24). Even when questioned, Jesus rejected divorce, according to Mat. 19:8, He said unto them, "Moses, because of the hardness of your hearts. Suffered you to put away your wives, but in the beginning, it was not so." He made it clear that Moses had to consider divorce as an outlet for bad marriages.

Because of the divorce rate today, many families are blended or extended to make up a household. I do not want to discuss the statistics on marriage and divorce, but I do want to discuss the struggles of the blended family. I want to examine the spiritual warfare that the blended family faces, and from a biblical perspective, we can see how to counteract some of the problems. Because we are a part of the body of Christ, it does not exempt us from the difficulties of having a blended family. The church, like the world, has a high rate of divorce and remarriage. Blended and extended family are a part of the church, the body of Christ. We must understand that blended and extended families need attention and encouragement to survive so that divorce will not be the only option. According to statistics, 60% of marriages end in divorce. But with the help of God, we know that failure is not an option. Through the power of God, we will succeed.

Many people go into remarriage blindfolded by their love for the person they have a relationship with and want to marry. There are so many others in the family that must be considered. Some people are a part of our past and want to affect our future. Then, some are in our present and must learn who we are. And some want to help us prosper in the future.

I lived in a household that was blended. My mother had four girls and no boys. Three of the four girls were from the first marriage, and the fourth daughter was from a relationship after the divorce. She married a man who had one daughter and two sons. My stepdad was a single parent. His ex-spouse left him and the children. Yes, there were hurdles that both my mother and stepdad had to jump. There were so many different personalities to deal with, including the ex of my stepdad. They had to be willing to commit, not only to one another but to every child involved in this marriage.

As my mother, I found myself raising a blended family. But times have changed a bit from when my mother was raising us. In my house, we had to have meetings and learn from each other how to respect one another. It was so that the family could blend peaceably. It made it easier for us to build a life and family together. In this idea, we had to make sure God would guide us through this walk as we dealt with the struggles of blending these two families. We had to go to God, who knew what we needed and how to combine a family with various issues.

This is Jesus Christ's invitation to us: "Everything has been entrusted to me by my Father. Only the Father knows the Son, and the Father is known only by the Son and by those to whom the Son reveals him. Come to me, and I will give you rest—all of you who work so hard beneath a heavy yoke. Wear my yoke—for it fits perfectly—and let me teach you; for I am gentle and humble, and you shall find rest for your souls; "for I give you only light burdens." Matt. 11:2730 (TLB)

Origin of The Family

Genesis 1:26,27; 2:21-23; 5:2

God is the creator of all things, specializing in human relationships and the whole human race. He is a family man.

God created the institution of family. God intended to have a family in the earth to reflect his image. So, let's find the meaning and understand what a family is. A family is a group of individuals living under the same roof, usually under one head. It is also called a household. Then, there is a group of persons of common ancestry. It is known as a clan, yet a family. Then again, a family is everyone in the same house or household. It is the house as a whole. The whole is the keyword here. A household is a social unit consisting of two parents and the child(ren) they are rearing.

Some other meanings and subjects can be called family. We will discuss the human family. We will discuss the history or origin of the family. We will also discuss the reality of the blended family. Anyone can say what they believe a family is, but we will see what God created a family to be. God (the creator of man, marriage, and family) started the first family in the Garden of Eden. God, after the creation of all things, made man in his image and after his likeness. After creating everything he did, the man found no helper or mate. God said, "It is not good for man to be lonely or alone." So, God put the man, Adam, in a deep sleep, took a rib, and made him a mate called a woman. The woman was called Eve, meaning life. God created male and female in his image and blessed them after his likeness. He commanded them to replenish the earth. Adam now had someone he could communicate with. God called their name Adam because they were one. God was the first Father to give a woman in holy matrimony. God, the creator of heaven and earth, got personal and up close when it came to Marriage for Adam.

Once God gave Eve to Adam in holy matrimony, he told them to be fruitful and multiply. They were to produce after their kind. Adam was not supposed to mate with the ape or the baboon. No other creature in the garden could meet what God required of Adam. He had to do everything else God had made in the garden. He had to produce something that was in his image and likeness. Every tree with fruit had a seed in it that could reproduce itself. So, God went into the man and took out a rib. He made it into the thing that could help him reproduce after his kind, the Woman, Eve. When Adam and Eve came together, Eve conceived. The family unit began right in the garden. Yes, the family of God began with one male, one female, and the children. God started a family by giving us an example of a family. In this family, tragedy stuck but did not derail God's plan for the family. Genesis 5 provides us with a list of ancestry names of those who would continue the family lineage of God even though Adam and Eve had other sons and daughters. God chose their son Seth. Then, from Seth, Noah and his sons were chosen by God to reproduce and replenish the earth; even out of Noah's sons, God chose one to raise his family, Shem. Noah had three sons, and through these sons of Noah, the whole earth was filled again with people. All the families of the earth spoke the same language.

As time passed, they came from the east to build a city with a tower that would reach to the heaven. The idea was to make a name for themselves. They didn't want to be separated or scattered. It was rebellion and idolatry. They had decided to erect a tower. God was not pleased with this. He came down to see what they had done. Being displeased with their action of rebellion, God confounded their languages so that they could not understand one another. Each family left that work and went the way of the tongue that they spoke. They left as God purposed and scattered out, building their cities. God separated through language.

God gave men different dialects to create families as God planned. It made different nations and tongues. I must mention that as we see the mind of God, his plan was for one man, one Woman, to create the family unit, which Adam and Eve did. Then, idolatry causes a separation in the family. Language became a barrier. It was God's plan. So now God must refuse what he has separated. He has to blend the family again. Blending means mixing or mingling to produce the desired result. It is to combine or fuse thoroughly. To unite or to go well together as to harmonize. It is what we expect when we are developing our families.

The Blended Family - What is a Blended Family?

A blended family is two or more families coming together as one in the union of marriage, adoption, or foster care and parenting. There is an enemy to family unity no matter what form your family unit is. This enemy brings chaos and confusion so that a household may become unstable and cannot survive. This enemy's name is Satan, the devil. He was in the Garden of Eden when Adam and Eve were there. With crafty and subtle speech through the serpent in the garden, the devil deceived the Woman, Eve (Gen. 3:1-6). Satan destabilized the harmony that Adam and Eve had with God in the garden that God himself had placed them in. When they found themselves, they were kicked out of their stable, healthy home and environment (Gen 3:23-24). Family does not matter to this enemy of all that is good. He will challenge the family. You cannot see this enemy physically, but you can discern that he is trying to take advantage of you and your family. You cannot fight with bullets and guns. No, you cannot fight with swords and spears. The battle must be taken to God in prayer to get the proper counsel and find the winning strategy. In every area of our lives, we are engaged in spiritual warfare, and family is not exempt.

Now, let's talk about the blended family. There are several kinds of blended families, as I have spoken of before. There is (a) marriage, (b) remarriage, (c) adoption, (d) foster care parenting, and (e) unwed parents with children of different fathers or mothers. One of the most intense conversations that we must discuss in this lesson is the (f) same-sex LBGTQ families. We can't avoid it. These families are a part of the fabric of this nation. As intense as this conversation is for the Christian community, you must know and understand same-sex marriages and relationships are still a part of the family unit. As of right now, same-sex marriage is the law. In June 2015, the Supreme Court lifted all bans on same-sex marriages and made it legal in every state.

Also, as we discuss blending a family, we must be aware of the fact that some children have emotional, mental, and physical challenges. It is very important for the individual who decides to marry someone with a child with such challenges to learn and familiarize themselves with raising a child with such a challenge. Love does conquer and covers all, but children with specific challenges can be overwhelming and hard to strain on the marriage. Many people make the mistake of entering into a marriage, and it will all fall into place. However, educating oneself concerning the challenge of the child who has the challenge is the best option of all. It is essential to create a healthy, thriving environment for the children from all parents, both biological and stepparents.

(a) **Marriage** is a form of blending families. It starts with him and her. They come together in holy matrimony, excited and in love.

However, this love will become challenging because many past household behaviors will follow each of them to their new life and home. Their job is not to create the home they came out of but to create their own healthy, stable home and environment. Home should be a place of peace and love. You must be careful of outside voices. They can irreparably damage the home. So, they must take the things they have learned from the home they previously lived in and fuse them to make a happy home for themselves. We use the man and woman to discuss Marriage because God's first couple to be wed was a man and a woman. The Lord formed man from the dust of the ground and breathed into his nostrils the breath of life, and man became a living soul (Gen. 2:7 KJV). And the Lord said It is not good for man to be alone. I will make him a help meet for him(Gen. 2:18 KJV). And the Lord caused a deep sleep to fall upon Adam, and he slept. He took one of his ribs and closed up the flesh instead thereof. And the rib the Lord God had taken from the man made him a woman. Adam said This is bone of my bone and flesh of my flesh. She shall be called a Woman because God took her out of Man. Therefore, a man shall leave his father and his mother and cleave to his wife, and they shall be one flesh (Gen 2:21-24). In many words, God said that when you leave home, establish your own house. (This very advice is good for those who are in same-sex marriages and those in monogamous relationships who are committed to one another without a marriage ceremony or standing before the minister with vows.) Establish your own house.

(b) **Interracial Marriage** has a bit of a more challenging role than that of a couple of the same race, ethnicity, or culture marriage. America is a multicultural nation. Interracial marriages are common in this nation, but so is prejudice. It is more ethnically diverse than most countries. Interracial marriages are blended families. Acceptance on both sides of the family is part of creating a stable and lasting marriage, especially from the immediate family. The couple's families must learn to respect each other and the couple's marriage. They must learn to respect their ethical and cultural customs and traditions. Their family's history can be worlds apart. In this, the couple must work extra hard to ensure that other family members' prejudices or negative feelings and behaviors do not interfere with their marriage. Children are not born prejudiced. Prejudice is something that is taught. Now, the task for the couple is to create a loving and peaceable environment for themselves and their children. It also should be the atmosphere they should seek to have for anyone who enters their home. The couple must establish their home with the traditions and values that they believe in. They cannot create their home in a certain way to satisfy their parents or any other outside person. They must establish their home to accommodate their unique difference in culture and traditions in the relationship and marriage. The goal should be for peace in the house and family. Prejudiced loved ones can make it very difficult to keep peace and harmony with them. Even Moses had to deal with the prejudiced voice of his immediate family members. God had to squash the ethnic and racial rant of Moses's older siblings.

Moses went to Midian after he fled from Pharaoh. Moses met the priest of Midian. Moses was content to dwell with the man (priest), and he gave Moses his daughter, Zipporah. And she bears him a son and calls his name Gershom: for he said, I have been a stranger in a strange land.

(Ex. 2:21-22 KJV). We even see that there was a cultural difference between Moses and Zipporah. Circumcision was an essential ritual in Hebrew tradition but not for his wife, Zipporah's culture. Moses had to keep the tradition of circumcision even if his wife disagreed. Now, on the journey, at the night's resting place, the LORD came in his (Moses) way and would put him (Moses) to death. Then Zipporah took a sharp stone and cut off the skin of her son's private parts, and touching his feet with it, she said, Truly you are a husband of blood to me (Ex. 4:24-26 BBE), Somewhere doing this journey to Egypt or after reaching Egypt Moses sent Zipporah and his sons back to Midian. Moses must have taken another wife, as we learn in Numbers 12:1. This made his siblings speak out, and their prejudice began to show. And Miriam and Aaron spoke against Moses because of the Ethiopian (Cushite) woman whom he had married, for he had married an Ethiopian (Cushite) woman (Num. 12:1 KJV). Whether this was the same woman or another wife, we see the prejudice of Moses' family against his wife (s). No matter what Moses's immediate family thought about his Marriage, God disagreed with their discriminatory behavior. Prejudice is nothing new in families.

(c) **Remarriage** is to get married over again. It is the marriage of someone who has been married before. It is when a person marries again when a previous marriage ends due to divorce or being widowed. We can only discuss remarriage if we discuss divorce. Because of the divorce rate in our society, we see more and more blended families. It is even true in the church. Pew research shows that Evangelicals, Christians, and Protestants have the highest rate of divorce than any religious group. Divorce was not God's plan for marriage. God instituted marriage. It is sacred to God. It builds homes, communities, and countries. The first mention of divorce was in the Bible by Moses (Duet. 24:1). Jesus had to answer the question of divorce (Mat 5:31, 19:7; Mk 10:4). In California, 1969, Ronald Reagan passed the no-fault divorce law, and divorces soared. Children are often the victims of these divorces. But, not every single parent is due to divorce. Some are widowed, and others perhaps never married but have children (maybe common law). Whatever the reason, some parents find themselves alone with their children. Marrying someone with children and you have children yourself is a task. It means that the two families have to blend into a unit. The two families have to now operate as one household. The children must get familiar with the parents' having someone else as a spouse instead of their mom or dad. One of the parents is absent in that new marriage, whether it be mom or dad. When I speak of absence, I mean that the parent no longer lives under the same roof as the child(ren). And because that parent is no longer in the same residence as that child, that parent can't meet all of that child's physical, mental, and financial needs (ren). It is impossible to be in two places at one time. Every adult involved must be an adult in the relationship for the children's sake. Indeed, if adults are about to blend their families through marriage should understand that there is more to consider than themselves and marriage. Depending on the age of the children, that transition can be smooth. If there are adolescents, teenagers, and young adults, then it can be a difficult transition for them. They would now have to adapt to the changes in rules and authority. The toddlers and the preschoolers do not have as much emotional struggle as the older children do. The toddlers and preschoolers will sometimes accept the new spouse with no problem. They will even go as far as to call the stepparent mommy or daddy. In dealing with adolescents, teenagers, and young adults, the focus has to be on transforming the house into a home for all involved. The objective is to bring stability and harmony into the home. We all want a healthy, well-rounded, stable home, no matter whose child(ren) lives there. However, in some cases, the children are under the supervision of three or four parents. It can be challenging for them to navigate through. Sarai thought the family was well until she had Isaac.

Sarai Abram's wife took Hagar, her maid, the Egyptian after Abram had dwelled ten years in the land of Canaan and gave her to her husband to be his wife. And he went into Hagar, she conceived, her mistress was despised in her eyes (Gen. 16:3-4KJV). Even though it was a polygamist family, the reactions were generally the same with the adults and children. And Sarah said, Who would have said to Abraham that Sarah has a child at her breast? For we, I have given him a son now when he is old. And Abraham made a feast when the child was old enough to be taken from the breast. And

Sarah saw the son of Hagar, the Egyptian, playing with Isaac. So she said to Abraham, Send away the Woman and her son, for that Woman's son, is not to have a part in the heritage with my son Isaac. This was a great grief to Abraham because of his son (Gen 21:7-11 BBE). Parents love their children and want the best for them. Ismael was not Sarah's son he was Abraham's son. The difference came in the children for Sarah and who they belong to. Here, you have the ethnicity and remarriage problem.

Now, look at Jacob's household, whose name God changed to Israel. He had a big blended family. Jacob had 13 children with four wives: 1 girl and 12 boys. His wives' names were Leah, Rachel, Bilha, and Zilpah.

Seeing that Leah was unloved, the Lord gave her a child, while Rachel had no children. And Leah was with child and gave birth to a son to whom she gave the name Reuben, for she said, The Lord has seen my sorrow. Now my husband will have love for me. (Imagine being the wife of someone you know didn't love you.) Then she became with child again and gave birth to a son, and said, Because it has come to the lord's ears that I am not loved, he has given me this son. In addition, She gave him the name Simeon. And she was with child again and gave birth to a son, and said, Now at last my husband will be united to me because I have given him three sons. So he was named Levi. And she was with child again and gave birth to a son. She said, This time, I will give praise to the Lord. So, he was named Judah. After this, she has no more children Gen 29:31-35 BBE).

Now, because she had no children, Rachel was full of envy for her sister. Then she said, Here is my servant Bilhah, go into her, so that she may have a child on my knees, and I may have a family by her. So she gave her servant Bilhah as a wife, and Jacob went into her. Bilhah became with child and gave birth to a son. Then Rachel said, God has been my judge, and has given ear to my voice, and has given me a son. So he was named Dan. Again, Bilhah, Rachel's servant, was with the child and gave birth to a second son. And Rachel said, I have had a great fight with my sister, and I have overcome her. And she gave the child the name Naphtali (Gen 30:1-8).

When it was clear to Leah that she would have no more children for a time, she gave Zilpah, her servant, to Jacob as a wife. And Zilpah, Leah's servant, gave birth to a son. And Leah said, It has gone well for me, and she gave him the name Gad. And Zilpah, Leah's servant, gave birth to a second son. And Leah said, Happy am I! And all women will give witness to my joy. And she gave him the name Asher (Gen. 30:.9-13BBE).

In the evening, when Jacob came in from the field, Leah went out to him and said, Tonight you are to come to me, for I have given my son's love fruits as a price for you. And he went into her that night. And God gave ear to her, and she became with child, and gave Jacob a fifth son. Then Leah said, God has paid me for giving my servant-girl to my husband. So, she gave her son the name Issachar. And again Leah became with child and gave Jacob a sixth son. And she said God has given me a reasonable bride price. Now, at last, will I have my husband living with me, for I have given him six sons. She gave him the name Zebulun. After that, she had a daughter, to whom she gave the name Dinah (Gen. 30:16-21 BBE).

Then God gave thought to Rachel, and hearing her prayer, he made her fertile. She was with child and gave birth to a son. And she said God has taken away my shame. And she gave him the name Joseph, saying, May the Lord give me another son (Gen. 30:22-24 BBE). Rachel had a second son; she called Benoni before she died, but Jacob named him Benjamin (Gen 35:16-18). Jacob's sons were full of envy, strife, jealousy, and thoughts of murder. It may sound like a family, you know. The adults must make every child feel loved and special, or it will cause division among the children.

(d) **Adoption**, foster care, and parenting are when one assumes the care and responsibility of children who are not their biological offspring. Often, grandparents and other relatives adopt or become foster parents, especially with the drug epidemic being so prevalent in today's society. Adoption is to take a child into one's own family legally and to raise them as one's own. Adoption commonly occurs in younger children (babies, toddlers). It is easier to mold and shape the life of the child. Adolescents and teenagers are more settled in their ways. In some cases, older children are a little bit more challenging. Some adoptions take place because of the loss of parents. Relatives may accept the responsibility of adopting and raising the child. Also, in the case of remarriage, the new dad may adopt the children he inherited from the new marriage. In most cases like this, the previous parent may be deceased.

Foster care and parenting is a temporary arrangement for the care of children neglected in one way or another. It may be by abuse or abandonment. They may come out of an institution. These children are in the home for stability and guidance and to create a family structure or atmosphere. Children from different homes may find themselves in one foster home. It is the caregiver's responsibility to blend this temporary family to the best of their ability. These children have different needs and should receive the same loving care equally. Whether adoption or foster care, the children's wellbeing is a top priority. Adoption and foster care have the same responsibilities. Moses was adopted and raised by a foster mom. The daughter of Pharaoh raised Moses as her own (Ex. 2: 5-10). Also, Mordecai took Esther as his own because her mother and father were deceased (Esther 2:7).

Adoption and foster care parenting is all about blending children into a home of adults who are not their biological parents.

(e) **Unwed parents with children of different fathers or mothers** also form a blended family. Even though the children may have the same single parent in the home, they may be for a different mate. This generation has the "baby mama or baby daddy syndrome." Most parents who use this terminology have two or more children in the home with different moms or dads. It creates a blended family. Because there is a different parent for one or more children, some characteristics of the absent parent may manifest in the children's lives. Each child will have some inherited behavior of the other parent. For example, if five children are in a home with five different fathers, each child will inherit something from that father. The man that fathered the child leaves biological traits and generation curses. Let's examine a family with different mothers and the same father. We will look at the family of King David. Now, there were sons born to David in Hebron. The first was Amnon, by Ahinoam, the Jezreelite; the second was Daniel, by Abigail the Carmelitess; the third, Absalom, the son of Maacah, the daughter of Talmai, King of Geshur; the fourth, Adonijah the son of Haggith, the fifth, Shephatiah, by Abital, the sixth, Ithream by the wife, Eglan.......

.......v5. And these were born to him in Jerusalem: Shimea, Shobab, Nathan, And Solomon, four by Bathshua, the daughter of Ammiel. Also, there were Ibhar, Elishama, Eliphelet, Nogah, Nepheg, Japhia, Elishama, and Elphelet, nine in all (1 Chronicles 3:1-9 KJV). The wives' names were mentioned, but the names of the (baby mamas) and the concubines were not mentioned, and also Tamar, their sister.

Even though the children knew they were siblings of the same father, they had significant behavioral differences.

Spiritual Warfare and the Blended Family

There are many things to consider when developing the right relationship in a blended family. Indeed, we are not all the same, from marriage to foster care and parenting. So many things can cause the family to have significant problems and destroy the family's relationship. Some things we must consider that can weigh heavy in the development of the family are (a) generational curses, (b) familiar spirits, (c) soul ties, (d) hexes of the exes, (e) lust, rape, and incest and (f) rejection.

(a) **Generational curses** and familiar spirits destroy any blended family. These behaviors and spirits travel from generation to generation. A generation is the overage interval of time between the birth of the parents and the birth of their offspring. The curse is the sin that travels from one generation to the next. So, the generational curse is the sin that passes from one generation to the next. The family we will examine is that of Jacob. Rebekah is the mother of Jacob and Esau. Rebekah had a brother named Laban (Gen. 24:29). Esau and Jacob were twins. Esau was born first, and then Jacob; Esau was the twins' elder. It was the custom for the elder son to get the blessing from the father before he passed. Isaac, the father of these young men, had eyes that had grown dim from old age, so he could not see. He wanted to bless the elder brother. So he called him to himself and requested that he cook him a meal, and he would bless him before he passed. Esau's mother, Rebekah, heard this, called the younger son, and instructed him to deceive the father. She did this so Jacob would get the blessing instead. So They deceived the father by putting kinds of goat hair on his arms to make him hairy like his brother. She had him put on his eldest brother's clothes so he would have the scent of his brother. She cooked the meat and bread and gave it to Jacob to bring to his father as if it was Esau. Then Jacob goes to the father as if he is Esau and puts the meal before him. Then, he proceeds to deceive him with instructions from his mother. Isaac questioned him, but he lied straight throughout his interrogation about who he was. They deceived the father; even when he smelled him, it was the smell of Esau. Rebekah taught her son the art of being deceitful to get what you want. But when the brother found out what he and his mother had done. He plotted to kill him after his father died. Jacob had to leave town because his brother wanted to kill him. He went to his Mother's brother Laban. Jacob worked many years for Laban and married his two daughters. Laban deceives Jacob by causing him to marry the daughter he was not in love with, nor did he work years for. He had already worked seven years to marry the youngest daughter. But instead, Laban tricked him with the eldest. Now fourteen years he work for Ladan to marry the youngest daughter (Gen. 29:130). Jacob's testimony to his wives was, " And you know that with all my power, I have served your father. And your father has deceived me and changed my wages ten times, but God suffered him not to hurt me. Do you see the generational curse? They are liars and deceivers. Rebekah deceived her husband. Jacob deceived his father. Laban deceived Jacob. It was all in the family.

(b) There is the **familiar spirit**, or, should I say, the family spirit. It is a demonic spirit that deceives as if it is working for God. In this way, they give their will to the demonic force that pretends to be an angel of light. They predict and promote things that have the signature of Satan on them. Familiar spirits seek to rule in the home by lies and manipulation. It will mimic God but is far from God's love and goodness. In the Old Testament, they are mediums and soothsayers. In the New Testament, they are called the spirit of divination. They do not serve God nor live for him. They speak as if they are the oracles of God, but it is Satan. Today, we call them psychics. The spirit of divination operates in them. They will even use the Bible as a reference point to seem spiritual and godly. They are in the community of the church and outside the church. Paul says to Timothy, You're going to find that there will be times when people will have no stomach for solid teaching but will fill up on spiritual junk food, catchy opinions that tickle their fancy. They'll turn their backs on truth and chase mirages. But you keep your eye on what you're doing, accept the hard times along with the good, keep the message alive, and do a thorough job as God's servant (2 Timothy 4:3-5). People with a familiar spirit have a form of godliness but deny the power of God to work and can cause destruction in any family, blended or not. God warned the children of Israel not to turn to psychics and mediums to get help. That will make you unclean before the Lord (Lev. 19:31). These people should not be giving your family advice from the demonic spirit that possesses them (Deut. 18:10-12).

Paul confronts the man and Woman with the spirit of divination.

Acts 13:5-14 (KJV)

And when they had gone through the isle unto Paphos, they found a certain sorcerer, a false prophet, a Jew, whose name was Barjesus: Which was with the deputy of the country, Sergius Paulus, a prudent man; who called for Barnabas and Saul and desired to hear the word of God. But Elymas, the sorcerer (for so is his name by interpretation), withstood them, seeking to turn away the deputy from the faith. Then Saul (who also is called Paul,) filled with the Holy Ghost, set his eyes on him and said, O full of all subtilty and all mischief, thou child of the devil, thou enemy of all righteousness, wilt thou not cease to pervert the right ways of the Lord? And now, behold, the hand of the Lord is upon thee, and thou shalt be blind, not seeing the sun for a season. And immediately, there fell on him a mist and a darkness, and he went about seeking some to lead him by the hand. Then the deputy, when he saw what was done, believed, being astonished at the doctrine of the Lord.

Acts 16:16-18 (KJV)

And it came to pass, as we went to prayer, a certain damsel possessed with a spirit of divination met us, which brought her masters much gain soothsaying: The same followed Paul and us, and cried, saying, These men are the servants of the most high God, which shew unto us the way of salvation. And this she did for many days. But, being grieved, Paul turned and said to the spirit, I command thee in the name of Jesus Christ to come out of her. And he came out the same hour.

God is concerned about family, and he needs no interference from Satan and his cohorts. It is human nature to want to know the future or what's ahead. So many people seek these kinds of demonic spiritualists to tell them of their future. But God is the only source that holds the future of every man, Woman, bot, and girl. Even social media wants to guide your life. They give advice that can be destructive to marriages and relationships. So, in either case, we must be careful with the advice coming from either source.

(c) **Soul ties** are connected by association and sexual intercourse. Many people are unaware that they may be soul-tied to another person. While some believe they are simply fond of a particular person, they may be interconnected at a soul level. The soul encompasses a person's capacity to feel, smell, taste, hear, and see. It embodies the emotional aspect of the person, encompassing their will, yearnings, and desires. In other words, it is the animated part of man. Man became a living soul when God breathed into his nostrils. He became alert, aware, with a will and a desire. No one is exempt from becoming soultied to another. Being soul-tied and be beneficial or destructive in a relationship. We often find someone we connect with and begin to spend time with them, whether male or female. It happens to our children usually. They make friends with someone, and before you know it, they want to spend all their time with that person. In your house, you are raising your children in the fear of God, but the person your child has tied himself to has no knowledge nor desire for God or church. Your child"s behavior and attitude may change gradually. So automatically, we start to blame the children whom they have befriended. But association brings on similarity and familiarity. In the similarity, they began to sound like the friends in speech. They also began to dress like their friends. The familiarity brings such a close relationship that it seems fanatical. The intimacy that is shared is unusual, even though sex is not involved. David found himself soul-tied to Jonathan. It was not a homosexual relationship, as some suppose, but a deep, binding love for one another. David finished talking to Saul. After that, Jonathan became David's closest friend. He loved David as much as he loved himself. From that day on, Saul kept David as his servant and didn't let him return to his family. So Jonathan pledged mutual loyalty to David because he loved him as much as himself. Jonathan took off the coat he had on and gave it to David along with his battle tunic, his sword, his bow, and his belt (1 Sam. 18:1-4 KJV). Soul ties are real. Constant communication can draw people closer and closer, just as it took time to build that relationship. It will take time to deal with such a relationship if it harms the family.

(d) **Hexes of the Exes** are very difficult for any household, no matter how loving it is. We know that hex has a negative connotation. But I used the word hex because some exspouses want only bad things to happen in the relationship of the former spouse. They may not go to the witch doctor to cast a spell, but the destruction they desire against the new marriage or relationship would be like casting a spell. Because they are so enraged and filled with anger and bitterness, they forget that the children in this former marriage are now involved in the new marriage. They should want a stable place for their children, but whatever hurt and pain they may feel outweighs a reasonable desire for that relationship. This person's mind is to see the former spouse's life destroyed without them. They cause as much trouble as possible in the former spouse's relationship or new marriage. They will not allow peace to be the portion of the former spouse. They seem unforgiving for whatever reason and choose to disrupt the former spouse's life in every way possible. They even use the children to be vindictive toward the ex-spouse. They will always see the negative side of anyone with whom the former spouse has a relationship and try to convince the children to feel the same way. It is done if they go through an unpleasant divorce for infidelity. The ex-spouse usually wants to repay the former spouse for their pain. This person wants to turn the children against any relationship the ex-spouse has. It infects the children so that they become disrespectful to the new spouse or person in the relationship. It is poison to the souls of the children. Hagar had a child for Abraham. Sarah interfered in their relationship and told Abraham to put Hagar and the child Ismael. Imagine Hagar being told she had to leave the only place she felt safe. She had to leave the man she knew protected her and her child. It would make anyone angry to realize you did nothing, but the relationship is over. It is impossible to believe that Hagar did not rehearse this in the ear of Ismael. Ismael was also old enough to know what the experience was like and had feelings of his own, as so many children do in the case of divorce. So, of course, we can believe the anger spilled over to Ismael. So many emotions flood the soul of the boy and his mother (Gen. 16:3-4;21:14-16).

Now, let's have a complicated conversation. We are discussing blended families. Today, blended families come in different kinds of households. We now have same-sex, legalized marriages. Some spouses leave home and start a new life with the same sex. It is more prevalent in women than it is in men. Even though this person may have been in a marriage of the opposite sex at first and children were born in this union, that person can become involved with the same sex and build a real relationship. You can call it lust, perversion, sin, or whatever. The facts are these people have become soul tied.

Some parents become very enraged over the situation and vow never to let the children of that union come around. But some parents want to allow their children to keep the relationship with the parent who is in that same-sex marriage alive and well. Younger children have no opinion one way or the other about the situation. They love their parents. Older children have their opinions about it. They can choose to continue the relationship or not. We have no opinion one way or another because we are talking about family. These choices are between the adults involved and the children. Even as some children are attracted to the same sex, and their parents disown them. So we know that in these relationships, there will be tough times and heartaches to follow. These people have souls. They can love, nurture, care, etc. All souls belong to God. There is nobody to discard as if their life is not important to God. We have to deal with the ills of society. We can't sly away from what is right before us.

Same-sex partners get married, have children, adopt children, and foster children. They have all of the privileges that a heterosexual partner and marriage have. They get divorced in the same manner as heterosexuals. They are raising children in their home. Their children are going to schools, churches, and playgrounds with our children. Their children have to deal with adjusting to a blended family when their parents separate or divorce. We, as Christians, can close our eyes and minds, but the reality is that it's all in our society. They are raising children in stable homes even though both parents are the same sex. They are teaching the children to be productive citizens in society. Their children go through the same pain and heartache aches we go through. I'm not asking you to agree with me. I am just sharing the truth of our society. We can not just accuse them of grooming children because children may come out of the heterosexual home and be attracted to the same sex. It has been as long as this earth existed. God spoke about it. Paul talked about it. The fact is that they are a part of this society.

(e) **Lust, rape, and incest** have been known to occur in the blended family. It is essential to understand that blending a family is a very delicate operation. When these families merge, there are more than just babies coming together. Adolescents, teenagers, and young adults are also involved in this merger. As children mature, their bodies change forms, and appetites emerge. If the adult has not created an atmosphere where everyone has a sense of family and boundaries, lust will present itself. The children see themselves more as a family than anything. If you don't cause the children to see themselves as related, problems can arise. You will find that lust, rape, and incest will become a problem in the family. Sometimes, when you have to deal with incest, you also have to deal with the soul tie that comes with it. The children must have that family relationship with the kind of bond of siblings. The sons and daughters must respect the adults, and there must be boundaries so everyone will learn respect for each other. Remember, new moms and new dads may be in love, but the children are learning to navigate the new blended family. Let's look at King David's family one more time.

After this, David's son Amnon fell in love with Tamar, the beautiful sister of David's son Absalom.

Amnon was so obsessed with his half-sister Tamar that he made himself sick. It seemed impossible for him to be alone with her because she was a virgin. Amnon had a friend by the name of

Jonadab, a son of David's brother Shimea. Jonadab was a very clever man. He asked Amnon, "Why are you, the king's son, so worn out morning after morning? Won't you tell me?" "I'm in love with Absalom's sister, Tamar," he answered. Then Jonadab told him, "Lie down on your bed. Act sick, and when your father comes to see you, say to him, 'Please let my sister Tamar come to feed me. She can prepare a meal in front of me as I watch her, and she can feed me.'" So Amnon lay down and acted sick, and the king came to see him. Amnon asked the king, "Please let my sister Tamar come and make some bread in front of me, and she can feed me." David sent for Tamar at the palace. "Please go to your brother Amnon's home," he said, "and prepare some food for him." So Tamar went to her brother Amnon's home. He was lying down. She took dough, kneaded it, made flat bread in front of him, and cooked it. Then she took the pan and served him {the bread}. But he refused to eat. "Have everyone leave me," he said. So everyone left him. Amnon told Tamar, "Bring the food into the bedroom so that you can feed me." Tamar took the bread she had prepared and brought it to her brother Amnon in the bedroom. When she handed it to him to eat, he grabbed her and said, "Come to bed with me, Tamar!" "No," she told him, "don't rape me! That shouldn't be done in Israel. Don't do this godless act! Where could I go in my disgrace? And you will be considered one of the godless fools in Israel! Speak to the king. He won't refuse your request to marry me." But Amnon wouldn't listen to her. He grabbed his sister and raped her. Now, Amnon developed an intense hatred for her. His hatred for her was greater than the lust he had felt for her. "Get out of here," he told her. She said to him, "No, sending me away is a greater wrong than the other thing you did to me!" But he wouldn't listen to her. Then he called his servant and said, "Get rid of her. Put her out, and bolt the door behind her." (She was wearing a long-sleeved gown. The king's virgin daughters wore this kind of robe.) So his servant took her out and bolted the door behind her. Tamar put ashes on her head, tore the long-sleeved gown she had on, put her hands on her head, and went away crying. Her brother Absalom asked her, "Has your brother Amnon been with you? Sister, be quiet for now. He's your brother. Don't dwell on this matter." So Tamar stayed there at the home of her brother Absalom and was depressed. When King David heard about this, he became very angry. But David didn't punish his son Amnon. He favored Amnon because he was his firstborn son. Absalom wouldn't speak at all to Amnon. He hated Amnon for raping his sister Tamar (2 Sam. 13:1-22). The father showed no interest in chastising the perpetrator. This family suffered greatly because of lust, rape, and incest. It will damage the relationship of any family.

(f) **Rejection** is something that has to be dealt with in the blended family. It will plague the household. The children will sometimes feel rejected because of the new relationship with the new family members. The new spouse may feel rejected because the children from the previous marriage may demand time from the dad or mom to be allocated to the new spouse. In interracial or different ethnicity marriage, there may be intense feelings of rejection because of the way the prejudiced family members treat the spouse. Sometimes, older children feel rejected because more attention is given to the younger children. It is even more so if the couple has a baby or babies are added to the family. So, there must be time for all the family members to feel important and cared for. Joseph's brothers rejected him because they were jealous of their father's attention and love for him.

Here is the account of Jacob and his descendants. Joseph was a seventeen-year-old young man. He took care of the flocks with the sons of Bilhah and Zilpah, his father's wives. Joseph told his father about the bad things his brothers were doing. Israel loved Joseph more than all his sons because Joseph had been born in Israel's old age. So he made Joseph a special robe with long sleeves. Joseph's brothers saw that their father loved him more than any of them. They hated Joseph and couldn't speak to him on friendly terms. Joseph had a dream, and when he told his brothers about it, they hated him even more. He said to them, "Please listen to the dream I had. We were tying grain into bundles out in the field, and suddenly, mine stood up. It remained standing while your bundles gathered around my bundle and bowed down to it." Then his brothers asked him, "Are you going to be our king or rule us?" They hated him even more for his dreams and his words. Then he had another dream, and he told it to his brothers. "Listen," he said, "I had another dream: I saw the sun, the moon, and 11 stars bowing down to me." When he told his father and his brothers, his father criticized him by asking, "What's this dream you had? Will your mother, I, and your brothers come and bow down in front of you?" So his brothers were jealous of him, but his father kept thinking about these things. His brothers had gone to take care of their father's flocks at Shechem. Israel then said to Joseph,

"Your brothers are taking care of the flocks at Shechem. I'm going to send you to them." Joseph responded, "I'll go." So Israel said, "See how your brothers and the flocks are doing, and bring some news back to me." Then, he sent Joseph away from the Hebron Valley. When Joseph came to Shechem, a man found him wandering around in the open country. "What are you looking for?" the man asked. Joseph replied, "I'm looking for my brothers. Please tell me where they're taking care of their flocks." The man said, "They moved on from here. I heard them say, 'Let's go to Dothan.'" So Joseph went after his brothers and found them at Dothan. They saw him from a distance. Before he reached them, they plotted to kill him. They said to each other, "Look, here comes that master dreamer! Let's kill him, throw him into one of the cisterns, and say that a wild animal has eaten him. Then we'll see what happens to his dreams." When Reuben heard this, he tried to save Joseph from their plot. "Let's not kill him," he said. "Let's not have any bloodshed. Put him into that cistern that's out in the desert, but don't hurt him." Reuben wanted to rescue Joseph from them and bring him back to his father. So when Joseph reached his brothers, they stripped him of his special robe with long sleeves. Then they took him and put him into an empty cistern. It had no water in it.

As they sat down to eat, they saw a caravan of Ishmaelites coming from Gilead. Their camels were carrying the materials for cosmetics, medicine, and embalming. They were on their way to take them to Egypt. Judah asked his brothers, "What will we gain by killing our brother and covering up his death? Let's sell him to the Ishmaelites. Let's not hurt him because he is our brother, our own flesh and blood." His brothers agreed (Gen. 37:2-27). When we start to show so much partiality to one child, it creates hatred for that child and causes the other children to feel rejected.

Overcoming Trials of the Blended Family – Generational Curses, Familiar Spirits, Soul Ties, Hexes of the Exes, Lust, and Rejection

I want you to know that all is not lost. There are ways to overcome everything that plagues the family. Overcoming is just getting the better of the struggle. We learn to master whatever the problem is. Sometimes, we are so focused on the trouble, issue, or situation that we can't see the answer right before us. Any problem can be apprehended if we follow the clear path to what we want to accomplish in the family. You must remember that You are not alone in this battle. It is a spiritual battle. There is an enemy to all that is good; Jesus said, "The thief comes not but to steal, kill, and destroy, but I (Jesus) come that you might have life and that more abundantly.

Ephesians 6:10-18 (TLB)

Last, I want to remind you that your strength must come from the Lord's mighty power within you. Put on all of God's armor so that you will be able to stand safe against all the strategies and tricks of Satan. For we are not fighting against people made of flesh and blood, but against persons without bodies—the evil rulers of the unseen world, those mighty satanic beings and great evil princes of darkness who rule this world, and against huge numbers of wicked spirits in the spirit world. So, use every piece of God's armor to resist the enemy whenever he attacks, and when it is all over, you will still be standing up. But to do this, you will need the strong belt of truth and the breastplate of God's approval. Wear shoes that are able to speed you on as you preach the Good News of peace with God. In every battle, you will need faith as your shield to stop the fiery arrows aimed at you by Satan.

You will also need the helmet of salvation and the sword of the Spirit—the Word of God. Pray all the time. Ask God for anything that is in accordance with the Holy Spirit's wishes. Plead with him, remind him of your needs, and keep praying earnestly for all Christians everywhere.

a.) **Knowledge** - Family History is critical because it gives you the individual's background. When you meet the family, you are meeting the person. All the red flags you need to be aware of and all of the great qualities. When the doctor sees a patient, he wants to know the history of that patient's family, including sickness and disease. We should like to know about a person and their family before we unite and commit to a lifelong relationship with them. Emotions and feelings are not enough to decide for a lifetime. Just going by feeling will fool you every time. It's not enough to feel right about it. You must know it's a suitable mate. In the Bible, we see the genealogy of the person who is the topic of discussion. When you read about them, you can always trace their ancestry and learn about the generational curses in the family. This does not mean becoming a private investigator. We are human. We all have something negative about our family history. But does the good outweigh the bad? You should know some history about the person you have decided to continue raising your family with. (example: how they feel about kids, sharing, spending habits, etc.) You must know that building a relationship with someone and both of you are serious could lead to marriage. It is essential to know some things about that person, male or female. Remember that one of the highest rates of divorce is in the Christian community. Even though God gives us a second chance at marriage or raising children, we should handle that responsibility carefully. Even when adoption and foster parenting are involved, it is a must that you have some history about the children's family and even the children. People are different, and we all respond to things differently. So it is good to have some history of the children that you care for. The necessary knowledge helps eliminate some problems while raising or parenting the children. Knowledge is just getting acquainted with facts about the person you are involved with, child or adult. Ecclesiastes 7:12 says Wisdom is a shelter as money is a shelter, but the advantage of knowledge is this: Wisdom preserves those who have it. We used to hear the saying that knowledge is power; believe it!

b.) **Individuality** is a must in the family as well as a unit. Often, we see ourselves as perfect. The Bible teaches us that a man's ways are clean in his own eyes. It gets us in trouble while developing our relationship with the new family. We know what the children should be, but are we what we should be? Everyone in the house is an individual and has their own identity. They have their own ideas and understanding. It is important to treat them as an individual that has feelings and thoughts. We know that rules and boundaries must be set to have understanding and stability in the home. I'm not suggesting the children do their own thing with no guidance. We must train a child in the way he should go. When we see the potential of each child, biological, stepchild, adopted or fostered, we are to steer that child in the appropriate path. That's the part where we deal with the children as individuals. They are all uniquely talented. Even though they have to deal with two separate households, the parents should agree on the best way to pull every creative ability out of that child. Blending the family takes time and effort, but it will be worth it. While creating boundaries with the children, we have to keep building the right relationship with the children. Coming together as a unit is necessary as well. That brings the relationship closer to a family structure. Yes, the children visiting their parents will want to be treated special. They need that individual attention, but it must not take precedence over carefully blending the family.

Jacob knew each of his sons. Yes, he loved them, but he never denied who they were. We can't be blind to our children, no matter how much we love them. So Jacob blessed each of his sons before he passed.

Genesis 49:1-27 (BBE)

[1] And Jacob sent for his sons, and said, Come together, all of you, so that I may give you news of your fate in future times. (Jacob would not hesitate to tell his sons the truth about themselves).

[2] Come near, O sons of Jacob, and give ear to the words of Israel your father.

[3] Reuben, you are my oldest son, the first fruit of my strength, first in pride and first in power:

[4] But because you were uncontrolled, the first place will not be yours; for you went up to your father's bed, even his bride-bed, and made it unclean. (Reuben committed the sexual sin of incest. He slept with Bilha, his Jacob concubine (Gen. 35:22). She was also his brother's mother.)

[5] Simeon and Levi are brothers; deceit and force are their secret designs.

[6] Take no part in their secrets, O my soul; keep far away, O my heart, from their meetings; for in their wrath they put men to death, and for their pleasure, even oxen were wounded.

[7] A curse on their passion for it was bitter, and on their wrath for it was cruel. I will let their heritage in Jacob be broken up, driving them from their places in Israel. (Jacob separates himself from these two sons because they were murderers. They killed men because of the rape of their sister (Gen 34). Jacob saw the wickedness in their heart as they tortured the oxen. Jacob curses their anger because angry men bring much destruction to the family.)

[8] To you, Judah, will your brothers give praise: your hand will be on the neck of your haters; your father's sons will go down to the earth before you.

[9] Judah is a young lion; like a lion full of meat you have become great, my son; now he takes his rest like a lion stretched out and like an old lion; by whom will his sleep be broken?

[10] The rod of authority will not be taken from Judah, and he will not be without a law-giver, till he comes who has the right to it, and the peoples will put themselves under his rule.

[11] Knotting his ass's cord to the vine, and his young ass to the best vine; washing his robe in wine, and his clothing in the blood of grapes:

[12] His eyes will be dark with wine, and his teeth white with milk. (Jacob sees that Judah will sit as a king with authority and power. His enemies he will defeat. He will be revered by his brothers. He will eat the good of the land and be prosperous.)

[13] The resting place of Zebulun will be by the sea, and he will be a harbour for ships; the edge of his land will be by Zidon. (Jacob sees Zebulun will be commerce. He would be by the sea where trade would be plenty. He would be prosperous in his dwellings).

[14] Issachar is a strong ass stretched out among the flocks: (Jacob tells Issachar he sees him living a peaceable life, calm and eased. He will live among his brothers in peace).

[15] And he saw that rest was good and the land was pleasing, so he let them put weights on his back and became a servant. (Jacob sees Issachar living a peaceable life, calm, and eased. He would work without complaint because he would be satisfied in the land).

[16] Dan will be the judge of his people as one of the tribes of Israel.

[17] May Dan be a snake in the way, a horned snake by the road, biting the horse's foot so that the horseman has a fall.

[18] I have been waiting for your salvation, O Lord. (Jacob tells Dan he sees him as departing from what was morally right and good. He would take his own path and not that of the family).

[19] Gad, an army will come against him, but he will come down on them in their flight. (Gad will be fought, but he will come out victorious.)

[20] Asher's bread is fat; he gives delicate food for kings. (Jacob says that Asher would be well fed for he will fare sumptuously daily.)

[21] Naphtali is a roe let loose, giving fair young ones. (Jacob tells Naphtali he will be of eloquent speech and swiftness. He will be blessed and godly).

[22] Joseph is a young ox, whose steps are turned to the fountain; 23 He was troubled by the archers; they sent out their arrows against him, cruelly wounding him: 24 But their bows were broken by a strong one, and the cords of their arms were cut by the Strength of Jacob, by the name of the Stone of Israel: 25 Even by the God of your father, who will be your help, and by the Ruler of all, who will make you full with blessings from heaven on high, blessings of the deep stretched out under the earth, blessings of the breasts and of the fertile body:

[26] Blessings of sons, old and young, to the father: blessings of the oldest mountains and the fruit of the eternal hills: let them come on the head of Joseph, on the crown of him who was separate from his brothers. (Jacob declares that Joseph had been a blessing to his brothers. Joseph will continue being a blessing to others. He is favored and loved by his father and God.)

[27] Benjamin is a wolf, searching for meat: in the morning he takes his food, and in the evening he makes a division of what he has taken. (Benjamin is blessed but not content with what he has is blessed with. He seeks for more.)

We know that Joseph showed favoritism to Rachel's sons. It harmed the relationship of the sons in the family. Also, the children of the concubines (maids) received less in the blessings.

Understanding each child and giving each an individual platform in the family helps bring stability to the family. Operating as a unit but yet having individuality. Every adult must be conscientious because favoritism will try to come into the home to cause chaos and confusion. It must be recognized.

c.) **Praying the prayer of faith** with a true heart. Men should always pray and not faint. Just believing that God is real is not enough. You have to develop a real relationship with God. No, not as some mystical being but as your Father. A Father who loves you and your family. A Father that is concerned about what happens with your family. Most of all, you must believe that God is a rewarder to those who diligently seek him. We know some children can be challenging when bringing the family together, especially from outsiders. During this time, you must understand that there is nothing too complicated for God; you must cast all your care upon him. God cares about your family. Prayer will be an essential part of bridging the family together. St. Paul says to be careful (anxious) for nothing, but in everything by prayer and supplication with thanksgiving, let your requests be made known unto God. Praying the prayer of faith is the key to getting the desired result. This prayer should be honest and of a pure heart. It would help if you had a genuine concern for the children and an explicit request for help. Not only should you pray for the children but especially for the adults in the families. Jesus promised to ask us, and it shall be given. Seek, and it shall be found; knock, and it shall be open to us. So, we must take the initiative to trust God to change the family for the better. If you ever considered yourself an intercessor, this will be one of the greatest intercessory assignments you will ever have. The first person you have to bring before God is you. Getting to share with God all of your fears and struggles, pour your heart out to him. As he heals you, you will know how to respond to every situation.

Ps. 66:18 If I regard iniquity in my heart, the Lord will not hear me.

Pro. 16:1-3 (GW) The plans of the heart belong to humans, but an answer on the tongue comes from the LORD. A person thinks all his ways are pure, but the LORD weighs motives. Entrust your efforts to the LORD, and your plans will succeed.

Hebrews 10:22-24 Let us draw near with a true heart in full assurance of faith, having our hearts sprinkled from an evil conscience, and our bodies washed with pure water. Let us hold fast to the profession of our faith without wavering (for he is faithful that promised;) And let us consider one another to provoke unto love and to good works.

d.) **Allowing God's wisdom and counsel to be your guide** in responding to the problems and situations that arise in the family. There is no counsel against the counsel of God. As you pray for each child individually, allow the Holy Spirit to minister to you and instruct you on what to pray for concerning that child. For we know not how we ought to pray, but the Spirit makes intercession according to the will of God. God knows the beginning and end of every person. As we pray, the Spirit leads us with word and groaning concerning the person we pray for. The inspiration that comes to us as we pray, inspiring us on how to handle the situations or deal with the problems, is only the wisdom and counsel of God. See, if we lack wisdom, we can ask God, who gives freely and does not rebuke us because we do not know how to handle our problems. God knows everyone in the household and outside the house who is a part of the family. He knows everyone by heart. God is acquainted with all our ways. Yes, every child and adult involved, from the youngest to the oldest. It may not change overnight, but we must remember that God knows our situation. Many people can give advice, but only God has the answer.

Proverbs 2:1-7 My son, if thou wilt receive my words, and hide my commandments with thee; So that thou incline thine ear unto wisdom, and apply thine heart to understanding; Yea, if thou criest after knowledge, and liftest up thy voice for understanding; If thou seekest her as silver, and searchest for her as for hid treasures; Then shalt thou understand the fear of the LORD and find the knowledge of God.

For the LORD giveth wisdom: out of his mouth cometh knowledge and understanding. He layeth up sound wisdom for the righteous: he is a buckler to them that walk uprightly.

James 3:16-17 For where envying and strife is, there is confusion and every evil work. But the wisdom that is from above is first pure, then peaceable, gentle, and easy to be intreated, full of mercy and good fruits, without partiality, and hypocrisy.

Hebrews 4:16 Let us come boldly unto the throne of grace, that we may obtain mercy and find grace to help in the time of need.

e.) **Respectful communication** is required to develop a good relationship with a blended family. There should not be any negative communication about the children's absent parent. It could lead to harsh feelings. Children love their parents. This is true even in same-sex families. Children often do not respond verbally to negative remarks about their parents, which could affect their behavior. Even though you and the ex-spouse could not see eye to eye and had to part ways, the children still love that parent. The new parent in the new marriage must communicate respectfully and try to get along with the ex-spouse. It may not be easy sometimes, but unity has to be the goal to build the home how you want it to be.

The practice of respectful communication must be in the house to make it a home. Communication is the foundation of a successful relationship. The tone and body language are also important. Often, everybody is still learning from one another in the house. Plus, there is the child or children who live outside the house who are a part of this family. They come to visit at certain times. The atmosphere in the home should be conducive to creating a place for communication. Yelling and screaming and cussing do not resolve anything. It only creates an atmosphere for bad feelings. So, we must work on our communication skills to build a blended family of love and respect.

Pro. 15:1 A soft answer turns away wrath, but grievous words stir up strife.

Col. 4:6 Let your speech be always with grace. Season with salt, that you may know how you ought to answer every man.

Everyone in the new relationship has to make changes and adjust to the new life with someone else. We as adults look for the children to change, but we must also change. We must practice walking in our new life with the help of God's delivering power. We as adults must make sure we have let go of the hurt from pain and of any abuse in the past. There's an old saying: hurt people hurt people. Our job is to ensure we deal with ourselves before coping with children. When King David realized his life was going wrong, He asked God to create a clean heart and renew his right spirit. We need to ask God this because change will come when blending a family.

Living Victoriously in a Blended Family

Many blended families are living victoriously, and so can yours if you are willing to submit to God and his word. If you can examine the person you see in the mirror, you can see many ways to change the direction of the family. Living victorious means harmony in the house and love in the hearts, even while concerns arise.

a.) **Goal** - The primary goal is the family relationship. Everybody must know that they are an essential part of the family. Each family member must understand that they matter, whether in or outside the home. Favoritism destroys family relationships every time it shows in any home. Stepchildren must not feel that there is favoritism in the home. Again, the goal is to live as peaceably and harmoniously as possible in the home. We must focus on the things and the people that matter. The adults must be cautious not to become deceitful and hypocritical in their hearts. This action will destroy any chance of a good relationship with the stepchildren. It would help if you were focused and clear on what matters, blending this family as one unit. The bigger the family is, the more needs there are. Every need can be met mentally, physically, materially, emotionally, and spiritually with God's help. The goal is to develop a loving family with care for one another. Everyone is acknowledged when making decisions that will affect the family. Family health and relationships must be the top priority. Not only do we consider the family or children in the home when making some decisions, but we also consider those outside the home. Teaching respect for one another, including the absent parent, is essential. Create an atmosphere to promote enough love for everyone in the family. Let us leave the pass in the pass and move on to a better way of building our blended family. All of this takes a prayer-filled life.

Eph. 5:21 Submitting yourselves one to another in the fear of God.

Eph. 5:22 Wives submit yourselves to your husbands, as unto the Lord.

Eph. 6:1 Children obey your parents in the Lord, for this is right. Honor thy father and mother which is the first with promise, that it may be well with thee and thou may live long on the earth.

Col. 3:18-21 .... Fathers do not provoke your children to anger lest they become discouraged.

Rom. 14:19 Let us follow after things that make for peace and things wherewith one may edify another.

2 Tim 2:22 Flee also youthful lusts: but follow righteousness, faith, charity, peace with them that call on the Lord.

Heb. 12:14 Follow peace with all men, and holiness without no man shall see the Lord.

b.) **Every selfish motive must be denied.** Self will always think it is right and must have its way. Self will not be denied. All the ways of a man (person) are right in his own eyes. Yes, there is a way that seems right to a man (person), but the end thereof is the way of death. It kills relationships and family, even friendships. So you have to work hard not to seem right all the time. You must admit when you are wrong and apologize for whatever. As hard as it is to admit, as a parent, that you're mistaken sometimes, it will benefit the family's growth. Plans may be interrupted due to the children not living in the home. Don't panic because your plans must change; pray, especially if it is recurring. God will guide you through the place of deliverance for the child or the adult involved. Sometimes, a feeling of guilt will cause parents to run to every cry that is made of the children who do not live in the home, mainly fathers. If your children are in the house, you don't have the feeling that lurks in the recesses of the mind of the parent who has the children outside the household. It is hard to deny self, but it can be done with the help of God the Father through his Holy Spirit.

Rom. 15:1-3 We, then, that are strong ought to bear the infirmities of the weak, and not to please ourselves, Let every one of us please his neighbor for his good to edification. For Christ pleased not himself, but as it is written, the reproaches of them that reproached thee fell on me.

Phil. 2:4 Look not every man on his own things, but every man also on the things of others.

Even as written in the book of Acts of the Apostles, it should be in our homes as we continue to blend our families. They believed with one heart and soul. They believed whatever they had was to be shared with others. So, in the house, everything is to be for everyone. Everyone in the home should get a balanced meal. Everyone is to get proper health care. Everyone should be shown love and respect. Every child in the house or outside the home, while trying to blend them, should get some chastisement when misbehaving.

c.) **Acknowledging God's power to change lives.** Know that you can handle every storm in the family with God's help. Some things happen that are out of our control. We can't faint or fall out over it. We cannot be responsible for the actions of others. We are accountable for our actions. Some children will rebel and do things that cause disagreements between the adults, but with prayer and proper communication, it will work out. As we pray, believing God for change in us and the children. We need patience. It does not happen overnight, but we will see results as we keep the faith. Believe in God and trust in his word. God is faithful. When we sincerely pray, he hears us. He is concerned about the well-being of our family. God is a family man. He is our Father. There is nothing you will go through in your family, especially your blended family, that is not common to people. Every household has some challenge. But what seems to be impossible will become possible with God. He is our Father. So avoid leaning to your own understanding. In all your ways, acknowledge God; he will direct you in the way you should go. Some people have a form of godliness but deny his power.

Learning to submit to God is a process. The first step in this process is to become a new creation in Christ Jesus. Romans 10: 9-10 says if you confess with the mouth the Lord Jesus, and believe in your heart that God raised him from the dead, you shall be saved. From the heart, man (a person) believes in righteousness. With the mouth, confession is made unto salvation. This is to everyone, male and female. The care of God is rich to all who call upon him. He means that whosoever calls on the name of the Lord shall be saved. God will come and see about you in your time of struggle. So, how in the world can a man (person) believe in such a manner? First of all, there has to be a preacher called by God. It should not be a political message but a message about Jesus Christ and the life-changing power he gives us by the grace of God. This message should open your spiritual hearing. The answer to the question is, how can they hear except there be a preacher? The gospel of Jesus

Christ has to be preached in your hearing. Your faith will rise and increase more and more as you learn about Christ. You can grow in grace and the knowledge of the Lord Jesus as the preacher teaches God's word. He comes into your heart to make you a new creation in him (Jesus Christ). Old things are done away with. All things have become new. So we put off the old nature and its corruption and put on the new man who is created in righteousness and true holiness. We do away with corrupt communication. So, we change and become the children of God. John says beloved, now are we the children of God. We do not conform to this world's behavior, but renewing our minds transforms us. How do we cleanse our ways? We must take heed of the word of God. We must hide the word in our hearts so that we may live according to God's word. We understand that change can happen in our lives if we trust God. So again, submit yourself to God and resist that behavior. Let us put it to practice in the house, community, and job.

2 Cor. 5:17 Therefore if any man (person) be in Christ he is a new creature; old things are passed away. Behold, all things have become new.

John 1:12 As many as received him to them he gave the power to become the sons (children) of God even to them that believed in his name.

d.) **Commitment to a prayerful** life will help smooth out the rough places in the family. Prayer is the safest way to deal with a blended family. It means that your life must be filled with prayer. You must keep the family in prayer so they will tolerate one another and love one another. Commitment to prayer will help keep the focus on the marriage and raising the children. We know that God can keep what we commit to him, but we must keep up with what God has given us to keep. Yes, we want to keep that blended family together in love. We must commit our families to

God. We must trust God to guide our families no matter how difficult anyone or anything tries to make it. God will help us handle the good times and bad.

Luke 18:1 And he spake a parable unto them to this end, that men ought always to pray, and not to faint;

Luke 22:39-41 And when he was at the place, he said unto them, Pray that ye enter not into temptation.

Romans 8:26-28 Likewise, the Spirit also helpeth our infirmities: for we know not what we should pray for as we ought: but the Spirit itself maketh intercession for us with groanings which cannot be uttered. And he that searcheth the hearts knoweth what is the mind of the Spirit, because he maketh intercession for the saints according to the will of God. And we know that all things work together for good to those who love God, who are called according to his purpose.

James 5:13-16 Is any among you afflicted? Let him pray. Is any merry? Let him sing psalms. Is any sick among you? Let him call for the elders of the church; and let them pray over him, anointing him with oil in the name of the Lord: And the prayer of faith shall save the sick, and the Lord shall raise him up; and if he has committed sins, they shall be forgiven him. Confess your faults one to another, and pray one for another, that ye may be healed. The effectual fervent prayer of a righteous man availeth much.

Prayer is simply talking to God. You make your voice heard in the ear of the Lord. Prayer is the request that you want to happen in your life and your family's life. Prayer brings peace and comfort to the person who is praying. When we pray, God's peace will enter our hearts and minds. Always remember that God is concerned about your blended family, regardless of its form. His concern is for all who are in the house and those outside the house who are a part of this family. And with the help of God, we will triumph over every obstacle that the enemy set before us. No formula can guarantee all the members of the family will cooperate peaceably, but prayer will help find a place of peace and hope. We will have battles to fight as long as we are here on earth and have breath in our bodies. You win some and even feel like you lose some, but remember that the battle is not yours; it's the Lord! Keep praying!

If you have not accepted the Lord Jesus Christ as your personal Lord and Savior, please consider doing so today. Believe in the Lord Jesus Christ, that he is the Son of God, that he was crucified for the world's sins, that God raised him from the dead, and that he was received in heaven, ever making intercession for us. Then you shall be saved.

I thank the Lord God of my salvation, the Great God Jehovah, for the experiences he allowed in my life. I am the Pastor of the New Hope Deliverance Ministries. It's not a large group, but it will enable me to love beyond my household. It is the most incredible blend that I can call family.

About the Author

Dr. Jennie Morris is a wife, mother, grandmother, and great grandmother who is passionate about family. As a woman in a blended family, she understands how the enemy tries to come in with division. She is also the senior pastor of the New Hope Deliverance Ministries located in Texas and has been in ministry for over 40 years. Just like her family is blended, so is the congregation she oversees. She knows that family was structured by God, and God loves family no matter the blend. She is an author and poet. Her education in theology can not compare to the experience of counseling families who are coming together to create a happy, blended family. Dr. Jennie Morris knows that with the help of God, all things are possible.

Resources

<u>Bibles</u>

King James Version

Bibles -Logos Software

Bible in Basic English

Wordsearch 12 Version

God's Word

<u>Dictionaries</u>

Merriam-Webster

TheFreeDictionary.com

<u>Google Online</u>

PewResearch.org